Written by: Naibe Reynoso and Giselle Carrillo   Illustrations by: María Tuti

Text and Illustration Copyright© 2021 by Con Todo Press

ISBN: 978-17362744-4-6 (hardcover)
ISBN: 978-1-7362744-5-3 (paperback)
ISBN: 978-1-7362744-6-0 (ebook)

Venice Sign Attribution:

The Sign is a registered trademark of the Venice Chamber of Commerce and is used with permission.

Publisher's Cataloging-in-Publication data
Names: Reynoso, Naibe, author. | Carrillo, Giselle, author. | Tuti, María. Illustrator.
Title: Courageous Camila : a story about finding your inner warrior / by Naibe Reynoso and Giselle Carillo ; illustrated by María Tuti.
Description: Los Angeles, CA: Con Todo Press, 2021. | Summary: Camila loves reading books about powerful warriors, but when her mom signs her up for a martial arts class, her knees buckle with nerves. Camila rides waves of excitement, fear and disappointment, until she finally taps into her "inner warrior."
Identifiers: LCCN: 2021913178 | ISBN: 978-1736274446 (hardcover) | 978-1-7362744-5-3 (paperback) | 978-1-7362744-6-0 (ebook)
Subjects: LCSH Girls--Juvenile fiction. | Family--Juvenile fiction. | Jiu-jitsu--Juvenile fiction. | Courage--Juvenile fiction. | Hispanic Americans--Juvenile fiction. | Los Angeles (Calif.)--Juvenile fiction. | CYAC Girls--Fiction. | Family--Fiction. | Jiu-jitsu--Fiction. | Courage--Fiction. | Hispanic Americans--Fiction. | Los Angeles (Calif.)--Fiction. | BISAC JUVENILE FICTION / Diversity & Multicultural | JUVENILE FICTION / Lifestyles / City & Town Life | JUVENILE FICTION / People & Places / United States / Hispanic & Latino | JUVENILE FICTION / Sports & Recreation / Martial Arts | JUVENILE FICTION / Girls & Women
Classification: LCC PZ7.1.R4925 Co 2021 | DDC [E]--dc23

Printed in the USA
Signature Book Printing - sbpbooks.com

COURAGEOUS CAMILA

A Story about finding your inner warrior

By Naibe Reynoso and Giselle Carrillo
Illustrated by María Tuti

CON TODO
PRESS

One of Camila's favorite things to do was going to the laundromat with her *mamá*.

While helping fold laundry, she would listen to *Mamá's* stories about her little **pueblito** in Mexico, and the fun adventures she had there when she was little.

Camila also loved peeking through the window of the martial arts studio next door. Watching the students practice reminded Camila of all the **warriors** she had read about in her favorite books.

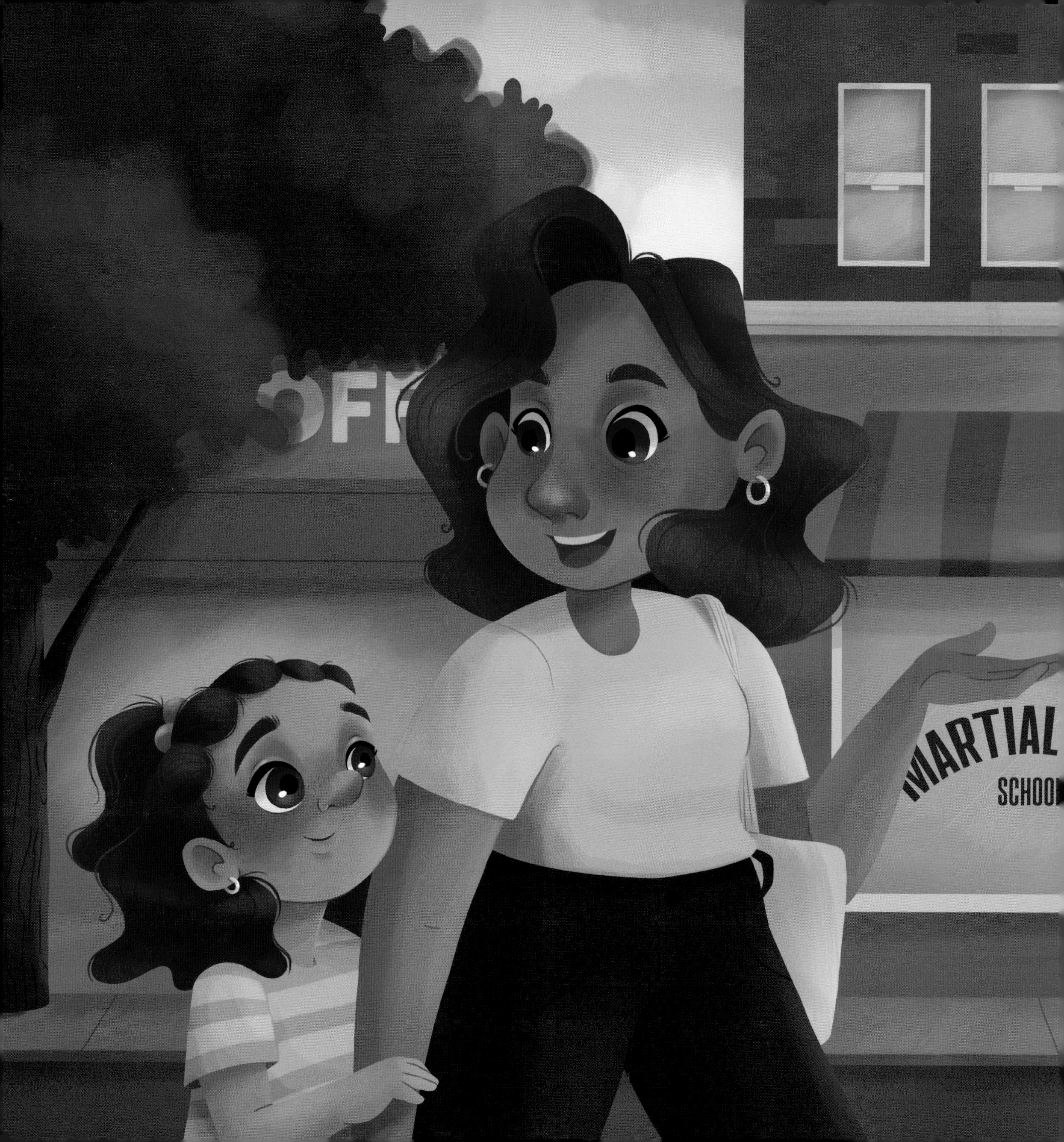
OFF
MARTIAL
SCHOO

One day, as they walked past the class, *Mamá* asked, "Would you like to try?"

"Me?" Camila responded with hesitation.

"Why not **you**?" said *Mamá*. "You shouldn't be afraid. You come from a long line of warriors."

And before she knew it, *Mamá* had enrolled Camila in Master Ren's Jiu-Jitsu class. On her first day, Camila learned that jiu-jitsu was invented so a smaller person could defeat a bigger person. The class was hard. Camila's knees buckled with **nerves** and she kept getting thrown down to the mat.

Camila told her *mamá* that she wanted to quit.

"Don't give up on you-yit-suu," said *Mamá* with her beautiful Spanish accent. "Everything takes **practice**," *Mamá* added as she handed Camila a ball of dough. "I had to practice for years to master *Abuela's tamales*. Before you know it, you will have one of those belts, just like the ones I'm tying onto the tamales."

Mamá was teaching Camila how to mix the *masa*, stuff the corn husks with delicious meat, and steam them until they were soft and doughy. But Camila's tamales were **floppy**, and still not as pretty as her *mamá's*.

Mamá's tamales were the best! On weekends, Camila enjoyed exploring the city while helping *Mamá* deliver orders. Today they were dropping some off at Mr. Kekoa's house. He lived in a beautiful house near the ocean. Camila loved visiting the beach. Even though it was close to her house, it felt like it was a whole **world** away.

"Aloha," said Mr. Kekoa.

Camila was happy to go to Mr. Kekoa's because she would get to see her friend Kailani, Mr. Kekoa's daughter.

Mr. Kekoa's house was full of trophies and pictures. In one of them Mr. Kekoa looked like he was on an ironing board, magically floating above the water. Mr. Kekoa looked so **strong** and **fierce**! Camila wished she had the same balance as Mr. Kekoa had. She could really use it in jiu-jitsu.

Their next stop was *Tia* Rosa's house. Camila liked going there because the **frutero** man was always out front. She would order a cup of chopped mangos with spicy toppings and lemon juice while she watched her *primo* Beto's fancy skateboard tricks.

Maybe one day I will conquer my fear of falling and be like my primo, Camila thought as she watched in amazement.

The next day, Camila was back in class and Master Ren had a big surprise for her. "I want you to compete in our next martial arts tournament!"

Camila felt so nervous her eyes got as big as two gigantic **tortillas**. I *don't know if I'm ready!* she thought as she raced home to tell *Mamá*.

Camila felt like there were a million butterflies in her stomach. "What if I'm not good enough yet?" she asked *Mamá*.

"*Mija,* **find your courage**," said *Mamá.*

"Remember when I was told that leaving my *pueblito* and coming to *los Estados Unidos* was something only my brothers were strong enough to do?" she asked.

"Yes," said Camila, nodding.

"I knew that wasn't true, and you need to believe in yourself," said *Mamá*.

"Remember, we come from a long line of Guerreras. Even your last name means 'warrior' in Spanish."

And so Camila practiced *every day* in her room to prepare for the big tournament.

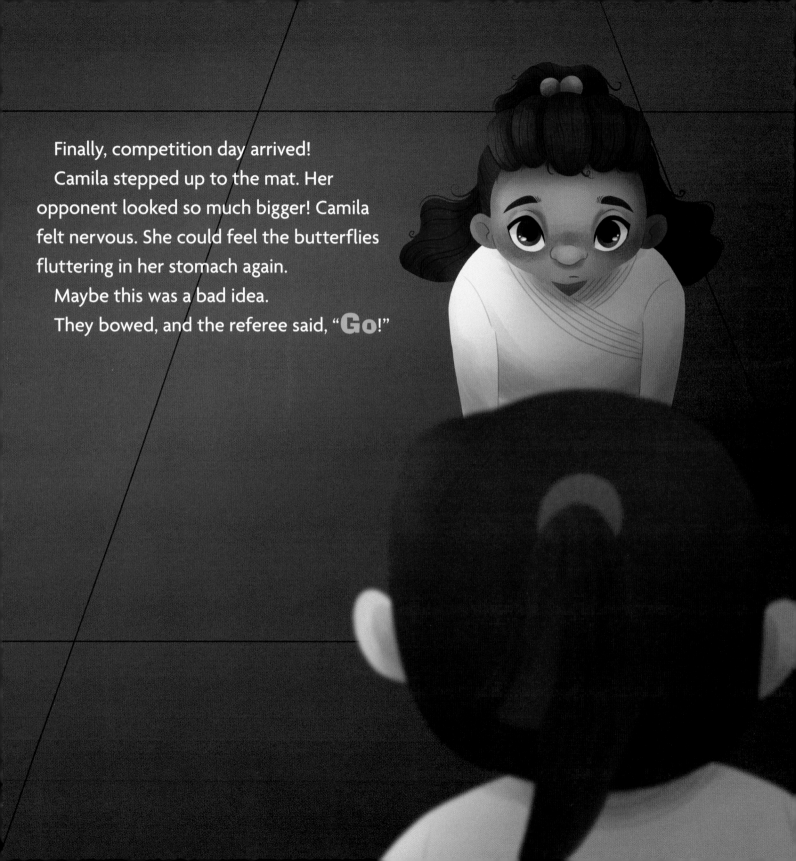

Finally, competition day arrived!

Camila stepped up to the mat. Her opponent looked so much bigger! Camila felt nervous. She could feel the butterflies fluttering in her stomach again.

Maybe this was a bad idea.

They bowed, and the referee said, "**Go**!"

Camila was tossed and turned.
Finally, the timer rang.

Camila had lost the match. She felt sad and defeated. She started doubting herself. Was she a *real* Guerrera?

But the tournament wasn't over. There was another match.

Camila looked over at *Mamá* who was
cheering her on from the stands.
  She remembered what *Mamá* had
always told her: ***"Find your courage.
Believe in yourself."***

Learning english

Becoming a U.S. citizen

GUERRERA'S TAMALES

BRAVe

Starting a business

Camila thought about all the stories her *mamá* had shared with her. How *Mamá* had the courage to come to this country and experience so many new things: Learning a new language, becoming a citizen and even selling her tamales.

Just then, she realized that *Mamá* was the **GREATEST WARRIOR** of all!

Camila summoned all the bravery she had.

And suddenly, she felt **COURAGEOUS**.

She was ready for her second match.

She took a deep breath.

She visualized herself as a **WARRIOR**, just like *Mamá*!

Just like the long line of Guerreras that had come before her.

She trusted her hands and feet to move
like she had practiced.
And just like that, the timer rang.
Camila won the match!

She stood at the medal podium as Master Ren awarded her with a new belt. "We are so **proud** of you, Camila. The courage was in you all along!" said *Mamá*.

"Mamá, I got my courage from you!"

And so Camila's family had a huge *fiesta* to honor her victory! And of course, they celebrated with *Mamá's* delicious, homemade tamales!

NAIBE REYNOSO
Co-Author *Courageous Camila*

I hope this book inspires children, no matter their age or gender, to explore sports or any other activity that may seem intimidating at first. I have seen first-hand how participating in sports changed my daughter Giselle Carrillo's life. (She happens to share the same name as my co-author.) She has been engaged in lacrosse since fifth grade, and was eventually recruited to play as a college athlete. But when I went to her tournaments, I saw a lack of Latinas on the field. Sports opens many doors for children and builds character and self-esteem. Unfortunately, there is still a huge disparity in Latina representation in sports at both the college and professional level. I hope *Courageous Camila* shows children that we all have courage within us; we just have to reach in and find it. The book is also a love letter to all immigrant parents, especially moms, many of whom sacrifice the comfort of their homeland and their own dreams, searching for a better life for their children. Immigrant parents rarely get the recognition they deserve for being strong role models for their children. They don't get awards, accolades, or the spotlight, but they bravely sit on the sidelines cheering us on. They are the ultimate courageous warriors!

GISELLE CARRILLO
Co-Author *Courageous Camila*

Be the person you needed when you were young. I hope this book is that story that I needed to read when I was a young little brown girl growing up in East Los Angeles. As the daughter of immigrants from Mexico, most of my young life was spent working to fulfill my family's dream: that their daughter would have a better chance. But at twenty-five, my entire life fell apart in the most tragic and beautiful way; I realized I had never lived for myself. So I went searching for my joy. And in that search, I was introduced to the ocean. Even though I grew up in Los Angeles, I never went to the beach and never really learned to swim. Surfing had always piqued my curiosity, yet I had never seen a brown surfer so I figured it must not be for me. But that mindset changed when I decided to conquer my fears and jump on a wave. It gave me back many things, including the courage I had lost as a young kid. And that courage led me to many other sports like boxing, weightlifting, Jiu-Jitsu and other joys like a new career, traveling, and starting my own grassroots community movements, Los Courage Camps and El Barrio Athletic Club. I grew up believing a little brown girl like me was not supposed to surf, compete in martial arts, or travel the world alone, but I realized we can always become what we were always meant to be, even if no one in our family has done it before. And I hope my journey shows little brown kids that they belong in these beautiful places too, because their skin is not a limitation; it is actually what makes them different and powerful.

Mamá's *Corn Tamales* Recipe

*While the recipe is meant for adults to make, of course, kids can help too if supervised.

Ready in: Approximately 2 hours ◆ **Servings:** 12 tamales

INGREDIENTS:

4 fresh ears of corn

1 package of dried corn husks (available in the Hispanic food section)

1 cup of milk

1 cinnamon stick about 1 inch long

1½ cups instant corn masa flour (masa harina)

½ cup sugar

½ cup olive oil

1 teaspoon of baking powder

¼ teaspoon of salt

1 steamer pot

COOKING INSTRUCTIONS:

Remove the dried corn husks from the packaging and soak them in water while preparing the filling.

PREPARING THE FILLING:

Remove the kernels of 1 ear of corn by slicing them off the cob with a sharp knife. Put the kernels in a blender or food processor with the cinnamon and the milk. Grind the mixture until the cinnamon is completely pulverized. Next, remove the kernels of the remaining 3 ears of corn. Fold the whole kernels into the mixture and blend again, but not too much so that the kernels are left a little chunky. Add remaining ingredients: corn flour, sugar, oil, baking powder, and salt. Mix with a large spoon for about 2 minutes, adding more corn flour if the mixture is too thin.

FILLING THE TAMALES:

Drain corn husks and dry off excess water. Open the corn husks, and fill each one with about 2-3 tablespoons of the mixture. Fold the husks, by bringing the left and right side inward, and then bring up the thin pointed end upward.

STEAMING:

Place the stuffed tamales standing up in the steam pot, with the open end facing up. Put water in the steamer and cook on the stovetop on low heat for 1½-2 hours. (Cooking time will vary depending on the size of pot and heat.)

SERVING:

Once the tamales have fully steamed, open the corn husks and place the tamales on a plate. To make your corn tamales more savory, top them with sour cream.

Special Thanks To:

Archana Patel

Claudia Botero

Gomez Jiu-Jitsu

Grace Niu

Liza Avanceña

Mason & Mila Pierre

Mayson Castellanos

Nancy E Cabrel-Perez

Natali Gonzalez

Los Courage Camps